MW00938182

LONDON

FOR KIDS

2018

TRAVEL GUIDE

☆☆☆☆☆

The Most Positively Reviewed And Recommended Places For Kids

EGP
Editorial

LONDON FOR KIDS 2018
Kids Activities & Entertainment

ISBN-13: 978-1544980164
ISBN-10: 1544980167

LONDON FOR KIDS 2018

Kids Activities & Entertainment

This directory is dedicated to London Business Owners and Managers
who provide the experience that the childrens and families enjoy.
Thanks you very much for all that you do and thank for being the "Kids Choice".

Thanks to everyone that posts their reviews online and
the amazing reviews sites that make our life easier.

The places listed in this book are the most positively reviewed
and recommended by parents and families from around the world.

" Knowing tips before visiting any place is always helpful "
We advise parents to find out more about the places, services and
individual programmes to determine its suitability for their child's needs.

Thank you for your time and enjoy the directory that is
designed with childrens and family in mind!

TOP 500
KIDS ACTIVITIES & ENTERTAINMENT
The Most Recommended by Parents
(From #1 to #500)

#1
Diana, Princess of Wales'
Memorial Playground
Category: Playground
Area: Hyde Park, Kensington Gardens
Address: Kensington Gardens
London W2 4RU, UK

#2
Hamleys
Category: Toy Store,
Children's Clothing
Average price: Modest
Area: Soho
Address: 196 Regent Street
London W1B 5BT, UK
Phone: +44 870 333 2455

#3
Swiss Cottage Leisure Centre
Category: Kids Activities, Climbing
Area: Swiss Cottage
Address: Winchester Road
London NW3 3NF, UK
Phone: +44 20 7974 2012

#4
London Aquarium
Category: Aquarium
Area: South Bank, Southwark
Address: Westminster Bridge Rd
London SE1 7PB, UK
Phone: +44 20 7967 8000

#5
Children's Book Centre
Category: Kids Activities
Area: Kensington
Address: 237 Kensington High Street
London W8 6SA, UK
Phone: +44 20 7937 7497

#6
Lydie Children Parties
Category: Kids Activities
Area: Clapham
Address: 4 Candide lodge
London SW4 6EP, UK
Phone: +44 20 7622 2540

#7
Dancing Cherubs
Category: Kids Activities
Area: Kensal Town, Notting Hill
Address: 242 Acklam Road
London W10 5JJ, UK
Phone: +44 7982 594001

#8
London Transport Museum
Category: Museum, Art Gallery
Average price: Modest
Area: Covent Garden, Strand
Address: Covent Garden Piazza
London WC2E 7BB, UK
Phone: +44 20 7379 6344

#9
Buzz Zone
Category: Leisure Center,
Gym, Kids Activities
Area: Beckenham, Elmers End
Address: 24 Beckenham Road
London BR3 4PF, UK
Phone: +44 20 8650 0233

#10
Quasar
Category: Arcade, Kids Activities
Area: Beckenham
Address: 94 Bromley Hill
London BR1 4JU, UK
Phone: +44 20 8466 7689

#11
Bunny Park / Brent Lodge Park
Category: Kids Activities
Area: Ealing
Address: Church Road
London W7 3BP, UK

#12
The Rainforest Cafe
Category: Burgers
Average price: Expensive
Area: Piccadilly
Address: 20 Shaftesbury Avenue
London W1D 7EU, UK
Phone: +44 20 7434 3111

#13
Topsy Turvy World
Category: Leisure Center,
Amusement Park, Kids Activities
Area: Brent Cross, Hendon
Address: Prince Charles Drive
London NW4 3FP, UK
Phone: +44 20 8359 9920

#14
Hornimans Adventure Playground
Category: Playground
Area: Kensal Town
Address: Southern Row
London W10 5AN, UK
Phone: +44 20 8969 5740

#15
Route 73 Kids
Category: Toy Store
Average price: Modest
Area: Stoke Newington
Address: 92 Church Street
London N16 0AP, UK
Phone: +44 20 7923 7873

#16
Bramleys Big Adventure
Category: Amusement Park
Area: Notting Hill
Address: 136 Bramley Road
London W10 6TJ, UK
Phone: +44 20 8960 1515

#17
V&A Museum of Childhood
Category: Museum
Area: Bethnal Green
Address: Cambridge Heath Road
London E2 9PA, UK
Phone: +44 20 8983 5200

#18
Thames Young Mariners
Category: Kids Activities
Area: Ham
Address: Riverside Drive
London TW10 7YJ, UK
Phone: +44 20 8940 5550

#19
Go-Kart Party
Category: Kids Activities
Area: Cricklewood, Kingsbury
Address: Mobile Go Kart North Circular
Road London NW2 7TE, UK
Phone: +44 7931 317949

#20
Gambado
Category: Amusement Park, Playground
Area: West Brompton
Address: 7 Station Court
London SW6 2PY, UK
Phone: +44 20 7384 1635

#21
Highbury Fields
Category: Park, Leisure Center
Area: Highbury
Address: Highbury Place
London N5 1AR, UK

#22
National Army Museum
Category: Museum, Art Gallery
Average price: Inexpensive
Area: Chelsea
Address: Royal Hospital Road
London SW3 4HT, UK
Phone: +44 20 7730 0717

#23
Fired Treasures
Category: Kids Activities
Average price: Modest
Area: Church End, Mill Hill
Address: 143 Dollis Road
London NW7 1JX, UK
Phone: +44 20 8371 6709

#24
Waterfront Leisure Centre
Category: Swimming Pool,
Leisure Center
Area: Woolwich
Address: 30 Woolwich High Street
London SE18 6DL, UK
Phone: +44 20 8317 5000

#25
Game Raiders
Category: Computers, Books, Mags,
Music & Video, Kids Activities
Average price: Modest
Area: Bexleyheath
Address: 4 Lion Road
London DA6 8NR, UK
Phone: +44 20 8304 4304

#26
Pizza Express
Category: Italian, Pizza
Average price: Modest
Area: Chelsea
Address: 7 Beauchamp Place
London SW3 1NQ, UK
Phone: +44 20 7589 2355

#27
Battersea Park
Category: Park
Area: Battersea
Address: Battersea Park
London SW18 2PU, UK
Phone: +44 20 8871 7537

#28
Funland At Trocadero
Category: Kids Activities
Area: Leicester Square
Address: 7-14 Coventry Street
London W1D 7DH, UK
Phone: +44 20 7439 1914

#29
Kidspace
Category: Kids Activities
Area: Purley
Address: 619 Purley Way
London CR0 4RQ, UK
Phone: +44 20 8686 0040

#30
Horniman Museum
Category: Museum
Area: Honor Oak Park, Sydenham
Address: 100 London Road
London SE23 3PQ, UK
Phone: +44 20 8699 1872

#31
Holland Park
Category: Park
Area: Holland Park
Address: Ilchester Place
London W8 6LU, UK
Phone: +44 20 7471 9813

#32
Cally Pool
Category: Leisure Center,
Swimming Pool
Area: King's Cross
Address: 229 Caledonian Road
London N1 0NH, UK
Phone: +44 20 7278 1890

#33
Rascals
Category: Leisure Center, Kids Activities
Area: Bellingham
Address: 5 Randlesdown Road
London SE6 3BT, UK
Phone: +44 20 8697 0043

#34
Dulwich Park
Category: Park
Area: Dulwich
Address: College Road
London SE21 7BQ, UK

#35
London Fields Lido
Category: Swimming Pool
Area: London Fields
Address: London Fields Westside
London E8 3EU, UK
Phone: +44 20 7254 9038

#36
Highgate Wood
Category: Park
Area: Muswell Hill
Address: Muswell Hill Road
London N10 3JN, UK
Phone: +44 20 8444 6129

#37
Etch Kids Drama Club
Category: Kids Activities
Area: Greenwich
Address: 141 Greenwich West Community
and Arts Centre London, UK
Phone: +44 20 8856 1021

#38
ZSL
London Zoo
Category: Zoo
Area: Regent's Park
Address: Outer Circle
London NW1 4RY, UK
Phone: +44 844 225 1826

#39
National Gallery
Category: Museum
Area: Trafalgar Square
Address: Trafalgar Square
London WC2N 5DN, UK
Phone: +44 20 0774 72885

#40
Super Camps
Category: Kids Activities
Area: Wimbledon
Address: Wimbledon High School Mansel
Road London SW19 4AB, UK
Phone: +44 1235 832222

#41
St John's Wood Church
Category: Kids Activities
Area: St John's Wood
Address: St Johns Wood High Street
London NW8 7NE, UK
Phone: +44 20 7387 4341

#42
Clown Town
Category: Arcade, Kids Activities
Area: Palmers Green
Address: 220 Green Lanes
London N13 5UD, UK
Phone: +44 20 8886 7520

#43
Virgin Active
Category: Gym
Area: Acton
Address: 36 Bromyard Ave
London W3 7AU, UK
Phone: +44 20 8600 9600

#44
King George's Park
Category: Park
Area: Earlsfield, Southfields
Address: Garratt Lane
London SW18 4GB, UK

#45
Rhubarb & Custard
Category: Kids Activities, Cafe
Area: Lewisham, Lee
Address: 164 Manor Lane
London SE12 8LP, UK
Phone: +44 20 8297 0035

#46
Super Camps
Category: Kids Activities
Area: Greenwich
Address: Blackheath High School Vanburgh
Park London SE3 7AG, UK
Phone: +44 1235 832222

#47
Coram's Fields
Category: Local Flavor,
Playground, Park
Area: Bloomsbury
Address: 93 Guildford St
London WC1N 1DN, UK
Phone: +44 20 7837 6138

#48
Science Museum
Category: Museum
Area: Knightsbridge
Address: Exhibition Road
London SW7 2DD, UK
Phone: +44 870 870 4868

#49
Hackney City Farm
Category: Zoo
Area: Broadway Market, Haggerston
Address: 1a Goldsmiths Row
London E2 8QA, UK
Phone: +44 20 7729 6381

#50
Tenpin
Category: Bowling
Area: Ealing
Address: Royale Leisure Park Western
Avenue London W3 0PA, UK
Phone: +44 871 222 3675

#51
Munchkin Lane
Category: Kids Activities, Cafe
Area: Clapham Common
Address: 83 Nightingale Lane
London SW12 8NX, UK
Phone: +44 20 8772 6800

#52
Tottenham Green Leisure Centre
Category: Leisure Center
Area: Seven Sisters
Address: 1 Philip Lane
London N15 4JA, UK
Phone: +44 20 8489 5322

#53
Swiss Cottage Central Library
Category: Library
Area: Swiss Cottage
Address: 88 Avenue Road
London NW3 3HA, UK
Phone: +44 20 7974 6522

#54
Juniors Plus, Hairdressers
Category: Kids Activities
Average price: Exclusive
Area: Carshalton
Address: 101 Stanley Park Road
London SM5 3JJ, UK
Phone: +44 20 8669 9999

#55
Smarty Paints Pottery Painting Studio
Category: Kids Activities, Children's
Clothing, Arts & Entertainment
Area: Clapham Common
Address: 85 Nightingale Lane
London SW12 8NX, UK
Phone: +44 20 8772 8702

#56
St James's Park
Category: Park
Area: Buckingham Palace, St James's
Address: The Mall
London SW1A, UK
Phone: +44 20 7930 1793

#57
Geffrye Museum
Category: Museum
Area: Hoxton
Address: Kingsland Road
London E2 8EA, UK
Phone: +44 20 7739 9893

#58
Winter Wonderland
Category: Amusement Park,
Christmas Market
Area: Hyde Park
Address: Hyde Park
London W2, UK
Phone: +44 30 0061 2000

#59
Greenwich Park
Category: Park
Area: Greenwich
Address: Charlton Way
London SE10 8QY, UK
Phone: +44 20 8858 2608

#60
Kebab Kid
Category: Fast Food
Average price: Inexpensive
Area: Fulham, Parsons Green
Address: 90 New Kings Road
London SW6 4LU, UK
Phone: +44 20 7731 0427

#61
Christmas Tree Farm
Category: Zoo, Kids Activities
Area: Downe
Address: Cudham Road
London BR6 7LF, UK
Phone: +44 1689 861603

#62
Trocadero
Category: Shopping Center
Average price: Expensive
Area: Leicester Square
Address: 13 Coventry Street
London W1D 7DH, UK
Phone: +44 20 7439 1791

#63
Tooting Bec Lido
Category: Swimming Pool
Area: Tooting, Tooting Bec
Address: Tooting Bec Road
London SW16 1RU, UK
Phone: +44 20 8871 7198

#64
Clissold Park
Category: Park
Area: Stoke Newington,
Stoke Newington Church Street
Address: Church Street
London N16 9HJ, UK
Phone: +44 20 8356 8428

#65
Mcdonald's Restaurants
Category: American, Fast Food
Average price: Modest
Area: Harringay
Address: Harringay Green Lanes Station
London N4 1DR, UK
Phone: +44 20 8880 2665

#66
Pottery Cafe
Category: Arts & Crafts
Average price: Modest
Area: Fulham, Parsons Green
Address: 735 Fulham Road
London SW6 5UL, UK
Phone: +44 20 7736 2157

#67
Museum Of London
Category: Museum, Art Gallery
Average price: Inexpensive
Area: Barbican, Farringdon
Address: 150 London Wall
London EC2Y 5HN, UK
Phone: +44 20 7001 9844

#68
Arches Leisure Centre
Category: Kids Activities
Area: Greenwich
Address: 89 Trafalgar Road
London SE10 9TS, UK
Phone: +44 20 8317 5000

#69
Antenna's American Diner
Category: American
Area: Norwood (West & Upper)
Address: 22 Westow Hill Crystal Palace
London SE19 1RX, UK
Phone: +44 20 8676 4316

#70
Giraffe
Category: American
Average price: Modest
Area: Kensington
Address: 7 Kensington High Street
London W8 5NP, UK
Phone: +44 20 7938 1221

#71
Pollock's Toy Museum
Category: Museum, Art Gallery
Average price: Modest
Area: Fitzrovia
Address: 1 Scala Street
London W1T 2HL, UK
Phone: +44 20 7636 3452

#72
Deen City Farm
Category: Zoo
Address: 39 Windsor Avenue
London SW19 2RR, UK
Phone: +44 20 8543 5300

#73
Sobell Leisure Centre
Category: Leisure Center
Area: Holloway, Lower Holloway
Address: Hornsey Road
London N7 7NY, UK
Phone: +44 20 7609 2166

#74
Finsbury Park
Category: Park, Playground
Area: Finsbury Park
Address: Finsbury Park
London N4 2DH, UK
Phone: +44 20 7288 1991

#75
Thames Barrier Park
Category: Park
Area: Silvertown
Address: Barrier Point Road
London E16 2HP, UK
Phone: +44 20 7511 4111

#76
Battersea Park Children's Zoo
Category: Zoo
Area: Battersea
Address: Battersea Park
London SW11 4NJ, UK
Phone: +44 20 7924 5826

#77
Richmond Viking Sea Scouts
Category: Kids Activities
Area: Ham
Address: Petersham Road
London TW10 7AH, UK
Phone: +44 20 3011 0740

#78
Highbury Pool
Category: Leisure Center,
Swimming Pool
Area: Highbury
Address: Highbury Crescent
London N5 1RR, UK
Phone: +44 20 7704 2312

#79
Play Toy Shop
Category: Toy Store
Average price: Expensive
Area: Homerton, Victoria Park
Address: 89 Lauriston Road
London E9 7HJ, UK
Phone: +44 20 8510 9960

#80
Young Film Academy
Category: Kids Activities
Area: Fitzrovia
Address: 20 Fitzroy Square
London W1T 6EJ, UK
Phone: +44 20 7387 4341

#81
Toys 'R' Us
Category: Toy Store
Area: Gants Hill
Address: Horns Road
London IG2 6BE, UK
Phone: +44 20 8554 4420

#82
Eat Play Love
Category: Cafe, Kids Activities
Area: Battersea
Address: 324 Battersea Park Road
London SW11 3BX, UK
Phone: +44 20 7738 9469

#83
Boden
Category: Children's Clothing
Average price: Expensive
Area: Ealing
Address: 16 -18 Hanger Green
London W5 3EL, UK
Phone: +44 845 677 5000

#84
Disney Store
Category: Toy Store
Average price: Expensive
Area: Marylebone
Address: 350 Oxford Street
London W1C 1BY, UK
Phone: +44 20 7493 7203

#85
Boogie Parties
Category: Kids Activities
Area: Westminster
Address: Children's Entertainer
London SW1P 3JX, UK
Phone: +44 7926 002777

#86
London Dungeon
Category: Landmark, Historical Building
Area: South Bank, Southwark
Address: Westminster Bridge Road
London SE1 7PB, UK
Phone: +44 20 7403 7221

#87
Coloring Pages
Category: Kids Activities
Area: Piccadilly
Address: 11 Vigo Street London, UK
Phone: +44 7963 235091

#88
Alessandra Tortone Mural Artist and Face Painter
Category: Performing Arts, Kids Activities
Area: West Hampstead
Address: Brassery Road
London NW6 2BE, UK
Phone: +44 7857 395591

#89
Kate Academy
Category: Kids Activities
Area: Strand
Address: London SW12 8EW, UK
Phone: +44 7983 734668

#90
Pixie Dixie
Category: Kids Activities, Children's Clothing
Area: Fitzrovia
Address: 40 Langham Street
London W1W 7AS, UK
Phone: +44 20 7631 2084

#91
Toys 'R' Us
Category: Toy Store
Average price: Expensive
Area: Brent Cross, Cricklewood
Address: Tilling Road
London NW2 1LW, UK
Phone: +44 20 8209 0019

#92
Boogie Parties
Children's Entertainer
Category: Kids Activities
Area: Westminster
Address: Anywhere within M25
London SW1A 0AA, UK
Phone: +44 7775 746229

#93
The Teeny Tiny Party Company
Category: Kids Activities
Area: Westminster
Address: London SW1P 3JX, UK
Phone: +44 7926 996772

#94
Frankie & Benny's UK
Category: American, Italian
Average price: Inexpensive
Area: Bermondsey, Canada Water, Rotherhithe, Surrey Quays
Address: Surrey Quays Road
London SE16 2XU, UK
Phone: +44 20 7064 9810

#95
Mile End Stadium
Category: Stadium
Area: Limehouse
Address: Rhodeswell Road
London E14 7TW, UK
Phone: +44 20 8980 1885

#96
Archway Leisure Centre
Category: Leisure Center
Area: Archway, Tufnell Park
Address: 1 Macdonald Road
London N19 5DD, UK
Phone: +44 20 7281 4105

#97
Zumba Stars London
Category: Kids Activities, Fitness & Instruction
Area: Euston
Address: London NW1 1NA, UK
Phone: +44 7970 799009

#98
Movie Parties
Category: Kids Activities
Area: Fitzrovia
Address: 20 Fitzroy Square
London W1T 6EJ, UK
Phone: +44 20 7387 4341

#99
Perform
Category: Kids Activities
Area: Angel, Islington
Address: 11 Prebend Street
London N1 8PF, UK
Phone: +44 845 400 4000

#100
Manor House Gardens
Category: Park
Area: Lee
Address: Brightfield Road
London SE12 8QG, UK
Phone: +44 20 8318 3986

#101
Perform
Category: Kids Activities
Area: Bayswater
Address: St Stephen's Church Westbourne
Park Road London W2 5QT, UK
Phone: +44 845 400 4000

#102
Victoria Park
Category: Park
Area: Homerton, Victoria Park
Address: Victoria Park Road
London E9 7BQ, UK
Phone: +44 20 8985 1957

#103
Liberty Development Enterprise
Category: Kids Activities
Area: Camberwell
Address: 9-11 Cottage Green
London SE5 7ST, UK
Phone: +44 20 7708 6932

#104
Studio Film School
Category: Kids Activities
Area: Clapham
Address: London SW8 2QJ, UK
Phone: +44 20 7538 8521

#105
31st Islington Scout Group
Category: Kids Activities
Area: Angel, Islington
Address: Noel Road
London N1 8HQ, UK
Phone: +44 7900 277167

#106
Zumba Stars
Category: Dance Studio, Kids Activities
Area: Angel, Islington
Address: 15 Liverpool Road
London N1 0RW, UK
Phone: +44 7970 799009

#107
Willesden Sports Centre
Category: Gym
Area: Willesden
Address: Donnington Road
London NW10 3QX, UK
Phone: +44 20 8955 1120

#108
Go-Kart Party
Category: Venues & Event Spaces,
Kids Activities, Go Karts
Area: Notting Hill
Address: London W11 4PQ, UK
Phone: +44 7891 838881

#109
Britain At War Museum
Charitable Trust
Category: Museum
Area: London Bridge
Address: 64-66 Tooley Street
London SE1 2TF, UK
Phone: +44 20 7403 3171

#110
Perform
Category: Kids Activities
Area: Battersea
Address: All Saints Church Hall 100 Prince
of Wales Drive London SW11 4BD, UK
Phone: +44 845 400 4000

#111
Studio 106 Art Gallery
Category: Art Gallery, Private Tutors, Kids
Activities, Art School
Area: Fulham
Address: 106 Dawes Road
London SW6 7EG, UK
Phone: +44 20 7385 5618

#112
Finsbury Park Cafe
Category: Kids Activities, Cafe
Average price: Modest
Area: Holloway
Address: Endymion Road
London N4 2NQ, UK
Phone: +44 7949 299474

#113
Perform
Category: Kids Activities
Area: West Kensington
Address: 87 Masbro Road
London W14 0LR, UK
Phone: +44 845 400 4000

#114
Finsbury Park Cafe
Category: Kids Activities, Cafe
Average price: Modest
Area: Holloway
Address: Endymion Road
London N4 2NQ, UK
Phone: +44 7949 299474

#115
Perform
Category: Kids Activities
Area: West Kensington
Address: 87 Masbro Road
London W14 0LR, UK
Phone: +44 845 400 4000

#116
New Malden Library
Category: Kids Activities
Area: Kingston Upon Thames
Address: Kingston Road
London KT3 3LY, UK
Phone: +44 20 8547 6490

#117
Wood N' Things
Category: Costumes
Average price: Modest
Area: Spitalfields
Address: 57 Brushfield Street
London E1 6AA, UK
Phone: +44 20 7247 6275

#118
Alessandra Tortone Face Painter
Category: Kids Activities
Area: West Hampstead
Address: 16 brassery rd
London NW6 2BE, UK
Phone: +44 7857 395591

#119
Olive Loves Alfie
Category: Children's Clothing,
Home Decor
Average price: Modest
Area: Stoke Newington
Address: 84 Stoke Newington Church St
London N16 0AP, UK
Phone: +44 20 7241 4212

#120
Latchmere Leisure Centre
Category: Leisure Center,
Swimming Pool
Area: Battersea
Address: Burns Road
London SW11 5AD, UK
Phone: +44 20 7207 8004

#121
Perform
Category: Kids Activities
Area: Barons Court
Address: St Andrew's Church Hall 10 St
Andrew's Road London W14, UK
Phone: +44 845 400 4000

#122
Wilkinson
Category: Department Store
Average price: Inexpensive
Area: Westminster
Address: Woodgreen Shopping City High
Road London WC2N 6, UK
Phone: +44 20 8888 3678

#123
YogaBugs Fulham
Category: Kids Activities
Area: Fulham Broadway, West Brompton
Address: Fulham Road
London SW6 1BY, UK
Phone: +44 845 899 7164

#124
London Pro Dance
Category: Kids Activities
Area: South Lambeth
Address: 208 Wandsworth Road
London SW8, UK
Phone: +44 7852 181239

#125
Queens Ice and Bowl
Category: Bowling, Skating Rinks
Area: Bayswater
Address: 17 Queensway
London W2 4QP, UK
Phone: +44 20 7229 0172

#126
Somerset House
Category: Museum, Art Gallery
Average price: Inexpensive
Address: Somerset House
London WC2R 1LA, UK
Phone: +44 20 7845 4600

#127
Bloomsbury Bowling Lanes
Category: Bowling, Karaoke, Bar
Average price: Modest
Area: Bloomsbury
Address: Bedford Way
London WC1H 9EU, UK
Phone: +44 20 7183 1979

#128
London's Bouncing
Category: Kids Activities
Area: Kensal Rise
Address: London NW10 5HJ, UK
Phone: +44 7894 080963

#129
Igloo
Category: Children's Clothing
Average price: Expensive
Area: St John's Wood
Address: 80 St John's Wood High Street
London NW8 7SH, UK
Phone: +44 20 7483 2332

#130
Activ Camps
Category: Kids Activities
Area: Wandsworth Common
Address: Emanuel School Battersea Rise
London SW11 1HS, UK
Phone: +44 7896 546067

#131
Studiotars
Category: Kids Activities
Area: Clapham, Clapham Common
Address: 17a Welmar Mews
London SW4, UK
Phone: +44 20 7627 5625

#132
Barnet Copthall Leisure Centre
Category: Leisure Center
Area: Hendon
Address: Great North Way
London NW4 1PS, UK
Phone: +44 20 8457 9900

#133
Club Petit Pierrot
Category: Language School,
Kids Activities
Area: Fulham
Address: 80 Mendora Road
London SW6 7NB, UK
Phone: +44 20 7385 5565

#134
Jakss Children & Babywear
Category: Children's Clothing
Area: Bow
Address: 469 Roman Road
London E3 5LX, UK
Phone: +44 20 8981 2233

#135
Barnard Park Adventure Playground
Category: Park
Area: King's Cross
Address: Copenhagen Street
London N1 0JB, UK
Phone: +44 20 7837 1512

#136
**Roos Academy
of Performing Arts**
Category: Dance School, Kids Activities
Area: Greenwich
Address: 141 Greenwich High Road
London SE10 8JL, UK
Phone: +44 20 8300 8815

#137
Rowans Tenpin Bowl
Category: Bowling
Area: Finsbury Park, Stroud Green
Address: 10 Stroud Green Road
London N4 2DF, UK
Phone: +44 20 8800 1950

#138
Perform
Category: Kids Activities
Area: Clapham Common
Address: St Luke's community Hall St Luke's
Church 194 Ramsden Road
London SW12 8RQ, UK
Phone: +44 845 400 4000

#139
Newington Green
Category: Park
Area: Newington Green
Address: Newington Green
London N16 9PX, UK
Phone: +44 20 7359 8474

#140
All Star Lanes
Category: Bowling
Average price: Expensive
Area: Bayswater
Address: 6 Porchester Gardens
London W2 4DB, UK
Phone: +44 7740 943372

#141
**Hot Steppaz Step
and Dance Club**
Category: Kids Activities
Area: Streatham
Address: 16 wellfield road
London SW16 2BP, UK
Phone: +44 7947 115278

#142
Baby Sensory
Category: Kids Activities
Area: Bromley
Address: Trinity United Reform Church
London BR1 3AQ, UK
Phone: +44 7590 013358

#143
The Tintin Shop
Category: Hobby Shop
Average price: Modest
Area: Covent Garden
Address: 34 Floral St
London WC2E 9DJ, UK
Phone: +44 20 7836 1131

#144
Squigglys Parties
Category: Kids Activities
Area: Muswell Hill
Address: London N10 1NJ, UK
Phone: +44 7531 238956

#145
Aquatic Design Centre
Category: Pet Store, Aquarium
Area: Fitzrovia
Address: 109 Great Portland Street
London W1W 6QG, UK
Phone: +44 20 7580 6764

#146
Activ Camps
Category: Kids Activities
Area: Barnes
Address: Barnes Sports Club Lonsdale Road
London SW13 9QL, UK
Phone: +44 7896 546067

#147
Perform
Category: Kids Activities
Area: Balham
Address: St Mary & St John The Divine
Balham High Road
London SW12 9BS, UK
Phone: +44 845 400 4000

#148
W4 Art club
Category: Kids Activities
Area: Chiswick
Address: Chiswick
London W4, UK
Phone: +44 7789 599931

#149
Westfield London
Category: Shopping Center
Average price: Modest
Area: Ariel Way London W12 7GF, UK
Phone: +44 20 3371 2300

#150
The Lion King
Category: Performing Arts
Area: Covent Garden, Strand
Address: 21 Wellington Street
London WC2E 7RQ, UK
Phone: +44 844 871 3000

#151
Royal Observatory
Category: Museum
Area: Greenwich
Address: Blackheath Avenue
London SE10 8XJ, UK
Phone: +44 20 8123 9911

#152
The Royal Artillery Museum
Category: Museum
Area: Woolwich
Address: Royal Arsenal
London SE18, UK
Phone: +44 20 8855 7755

#153
Pirate's Playhouse
Category: Playground
Area: Finsbury Park, Manor House
Address: 271 Green Lanes
London N4 2HA, UK
Phone: +44 20 8800 1771

#154
After Noah
Category: Antiques, Toy Store,
Furniture Store
Average price: Expensive
Area: Angel, Islington
Address: 121 Upper Street
London N1 1QP, UK
Phone: +44 20 7359 4281

#155
Avenue Q
Category: Performing Arts
Area: Westminster
Address: St Martins Lane
London SW1P 3BU, UK
Phone: +44 20 7434 7584

#156
Sasti Children & Babywear
Category: Children's Clothing
Area: Kensal Town
Address: 281 Portobello Road
London W10 5TZ, UK
Phone: +44 20 8960 1125

#157
Acacia Children's Centre Children Centre Services
Category: Kids Activities
Area: Leytonstone
Address: 8 Cathall Road
London E11 4LF, UK
Phone: +44 20 8496 2960

#158
Sylvanian Families
Category: Toy Store
Average price: Inexpensive
Area: Highbury
Address: 68 Mountgrove Road
London N5 2LT, UK
Phone: +44 20 7226 1329

#159
Bouncy Apple
Category: Kids Activities
Area: Mortlake
Address: Ormonde Road
London SW14, UK
Phone: +44 7570 793113

#160
Royal Air Force Museum
Category: Museum
Area: Colindale
Address: Grahame Park Way
London NW9 5LL, UK
Phone: +44 20 8205 2266

#161
The Kids' Kitchen
Category: Kids Activities, Food
Area: Totteridge
Address: London N20, UK
Phone: +44 7976 268520

#162
Peckham Rye Park & Common
Category: Park
Area: Nunhead, Peckham Rye
Address: homestall road
London SE15 3AB, UK
Phone: +44 20 7525 2000

#163
The Kids' Kitchen
Category: Kids Activities
Area: Totteridge, Whetstone
Address: 38 Oakleigh Avenue
London N20 9JJ, UK
Phone: +44 7976 268520

#164
Arts & Vintage
Category: Antiques, Gift Shop
Area: Highgate
Address: 263 Archway Road
London N6 5BS, UK
Phone: +44 7904 591698

#165
Victoria Park Books
Category: Bookstore
Average price: Modest
Area: Homerton, Victoria Park
Address: 174 Victoria Park Rd
London E9 7HD, UK
Phone: +44 20 8986 1124

#166
Bouncy Castles London
Category: Kids Activities, Arts & Entertainment
Area: Leytonstone
Address: High Road Leytonstone
London, UK
Phone: +44 20 7639 9295

#167
Stratford InShops Shopping Centre
Category: Shopping Center
Average price: Modest
Area: 70-73 The Mall
London E15 1XQ, UK
Phone: +44 20 8503 1531

#168
Lewisham Deaf Children's Society
Category: Kids Activities
Area: Forest Hill
Address: Kilmorie Road
London SE23, UK
Phone: +44 7946 898931

#169
Carluccio's
Category: Italian
Average price: Expensive
Area: Canary Wharf, Isle of Dogs
Address: 2 Nash Court
London E14 5AJ, UK
Phone: +44 20 7719 1749

#170
Stables Market
Category: Shopping Center
Average price: Modest
Area: Camden Town, Chalk Farm
Address: Chalk Farm Road
London NW1 8AH, UK
Phone: +44 20 7485 5511

#171
The Tokei Centre
Category: Gym, Martial Arts
Area: London Bridge
Address: 28 Magdalen Street
London SE1 2ER, UK
Phone: +44 20 7403 5979

#172
**The Creation Station Finchley
to Primrose Hill**
Category: Kids Activities
Area: Woodside Park
Address: 13 Holdenhurst Avenue
London N12 0JA, UK
Phone: +44 7931 531596

#173
**Kew Little Pigs
Micro Pigs London**
Category: Kids Activities, Education,
Mass Media, Pet Store
Area: Kew
Address: Dudley rd
London TW9, UK
Phone: +44 7904 617650

#174
Ironmonger Row Baths
Category: Gym, Leisure Center
Average price: Modest
Area: North Finchley
Address: 1 Norman Street
London EC1V 3AA, UK
Phone: +44 20 3642 5520

#175
Longfield Pottery Studio
Category: Kids Activities
Area: Richmond Park
Address: 3B Uplands Close
London SW14 7AS, UK
Phone: +44 20 8878 2226

#176
**Harry Potter Tour
Muggle Tours Walk**
Category: Tours
Area: The City, London Bridge
Address: London Bridge
London SE1, UK
Phone: +44 7914 151041

#177
Beautiful Skin Expertsz
Category: Kids Activities
Area: Ealing
Address: Ealing
London W5 4QT, UK
Phone: +44 7407 438954

#178
The Little White Company
Category: Children's Clothing
Average price: Expensive
Address: 90 Marylebone High St
London W1U 4QZ, UK
Phone: +44 20 7486 7550

#179
Littlechef-Bigchef
Category: Kids Activities
Area: Richmond Upon Thames
Address: 52 georges road
London TW9 2LE, UK
Phone: +44 7828 878683

#180
Oh Baby London
Category: Children's Clothing
Average price: Modest
Area: Brick Lane, Shoreditch
Address: 162 Brick Lane
London E1 6RU, UK
Phone: +44 20 7247 4949

#181
CoffeeMAX
Category: Cafe, Italian
Area: Upper Tooting
Address: 242 Upper Tooting Road
London SW17 7EX, UK
Phone: +44 20 8767 9892

#182
Hamleys
Category: Toy Store
Average price: Expensive
Address: Pancras Road
London NW1 2QP, UK
Phone: +44 20 7713 0889

#183
Stationers Park
Category: Park
Area: Hornsey Vale
Address: Mayfield Road
London N8 9LP, UK
Phone: +44 20 8489 0000

#184
Tantrum, Children's Hairdressing
Category: Hair Salon, Kids Activities
Area: Chelsea
Address: 398 Kings Road
London SW10 0LJ, UK
Phone: +44 20 7376 3966

#185
Amore Arts
Category: Specialty School,
Kids Activities
Area: Edgware
Address: 11 Eversfield Gardens
London NW7 2AE, UK
Phone: +44 7565 105179

#186
Perform
Category: Specialty School,
Kids Activities
Area: Belsize Park
Address: The Hall Senior School 23
Crossfield Road London NW3 4NU, UK
Phone: +44 845 400 4000

#187
The Little White Company
Category: Children's Clothing
Average price: Expensive
Area: Marylebone
Address: 90 Marylebone High St
London W1U 4QZ, UK
Phone: +44 20 7486 7550

#188
Museum In Docklands Project
Category: Museum
Area: Canary Wharf, Isle of Dogs, Poplar
Address: West India Qy North Hertsmere
Road London E14 4AB, UK
Phone: +44 870 444 3855

#189
ButterflyKids Model Agency
Category: Kids Activities
Area: Thornton Heath
Address: day lewis house
London CR7 7EQ, UK
Phone: +44 20 8406 0860

#190
Eden MObile Creche
Category: Arts & Crafts, Kids Activities
Area: East Ham
Address: Women Business Centre
London E6 3PA, UK
Phone: +44 7804 358590

#191
Azzuro
Category: Italian
Average price: Modest
Area: Southwark, Waterloo
Address: Sutton Walk
London W1D 4AD, UK
Phone: +44 20 7620 1300

#192
Postmark
Category: Cards & Stationery
Area: Balham
Address: 123a Balham High Rd
London SW12 9AR, UK
Phone: +44 20 8675 7272

#193
Party SuperStore
Category: Costumes, Party Supplies,
Wholesale Store
Average price: Modest
Area: Battersea, Clapham
Address: 274 Lavender Hill
London SW11 1LJ, UK
Phone: +44 20 7924 3210

#194
Street/Hip Hop Dance Classes
Category: Dance School, Kids Activities
Area: Croydon
Address: 164 Portland road
London SE25, UK
Phone: +44 7534 643816

#195
Mrs Kibbles Olde Sweet Shoppe
Category: Candy Store
Average price: Inexpensive
Area: Soho
Address: 57a Brewer Street
London W1F 9UL, UK
Phone: +44 20 7734 6633

#196
Pizza Express
Category: Pizza, Italian
Average price: Modest
Area: Wapping
Address: 78-80 Wapping Lane
London E1W 2RT, UK
Phone: +44 20 7481 8436

#197
Roos Academy
of Performing Arts
Category: Dance School, Kids Activities
Area: Woolwich
Address: Bushmoor Crescent
London SE18 3EG, UK
Phone: +44 20 8298 0430

#198
Igloo Kids
Category: Toy Store, Baby Gear & Furniture,
Children's Clothing
Average price: Expensive
Area: Angel, Islington
Address: 300 Upper Street
London N1 2TU, UK
Phone: +44 20 7354 7300

#199
Budsara
Category: Thai
Average price: Modest
Area: Chiswick
Address: 99 Chiswick High Road
London W4 2ED, UK
Phone: +44 20 8995 5774

#200
Cartoon Museum
Category: Museum
Area: Bloomsbury
Address: 35 Little Russell St
London WC1A 2HH, UK
Phone: +44 20 7580 8155

#201
Lipa 4:19 Wanstead
Category: Dance School, Kids Activities
Area: Wanstead
Address: within Wanstead High School
London E11, UK
Phone: +44 20 8472 8845

#202
Madame Tussaud's
Category: Museum
Average price: Modest
Area: Regent's Park
Address: Marylebone Road
London NW1 5LR, UK
Phone: +44 870 999 0046

#203
Kensington Gardens
Category: Park
Area: South Kensington
Address: Thurloe Place
London SW7 2RZ, UK
Phone: +44 20 7298 2000

#204
Kenwood House
Category: Art Gallery, Local Flavor
Average price: Modest
Area: Hampstead Village
Address: Hampstead Lane
London NW3 7JR, UK
Phone: +44 870 333 1181

#205
Somerset House Ice Rink
Category: Skating Rinks
Area: Strand
Address: The Strand
London WC2R 1LA, UK
Phone: +44 20 7845 4600

#206
Geeta's Childrens Wear
Category: Children's Clothing
Area: Upton Park
Address: 261 Green Street
London E7 8LJ, UK
Phone: +44 20 8552 4873

#207
Chiswick House Gardens
Category: Park
Area: Chiswick
Address: Burlington Lane
London W4 2RP, UK
Phone: +44 20 8995 0508

#208
Perform
Category: Kids Activities
Area: Barnes
Address: Barnes Mthodist Church Hall
Station Road London SW13 0NH, UK
Phone: +44 845 400 4000

#209
Soho Square
Category: Park
Area: Soho
Address: 1 Soho Square
London W1D 3JA, UK
Phone: +44 20 7641 5271

#210
Craggy Island Indoor Climbing,
Bouldering and Caving Centre
Category: Climbing
Area: Carshalton
Address: Woodmansterne Road
London SM5 4AN, UK
Phone: +44 844 880 8866

#211
Il Pagliaccio Restaurant
Category: Italian
Average price: Inexpensive
Area: Fulham
Address: 184 Wandsworth Bridge Road
London SW6 2UF, UK
Phone: +44 20 7371 5253

#212
Putney Leisure Centre
Category: Leisure Center, Gym,
Swimming Pool
Area: Roehampton
Address: Dryburgh Road
London SW15 1BL, UK
Phone: +44 20 8785 0388

#213
Namco Funscape
Category: Arcade, Karaoke, Bowling
Average price: Expensive
Area: South Bank, Southwark
Address: Westminster Bridge Rd
London SE1 7PB, UK
Phone: +44 20 7967 1066

#214
LCF Jazz-Mataz - Mike Thacker
Category: Kids Activities
Area: Harrow & Wealdstone
Address: London HA1 2JX, UK
Phone: +44 20 8621 7521

#215
Childcare Voucher Solutions
Category: Kids Activities
Area: Gants Hill
Address: 86 Beehive Lane
London IG4 5EG, UK
Phone: +44 845 601 6020

#216
Nando's
Category: Portuguese
Average price: Inexpensive
Area: Stratford
Address: Westfield Shopping Centre
London E14 5, UK
Phone: +44 20 8519 4459

#217
Kidz Adventure Zone
Category: Kids Activities
Area: Alexandra Palace, Wood Green
Address: 2 Coburg Road
London N22 6UJ, UK
Phone: +44 20 8881 9737

#218
Pizza Hut
Category: Pizza
Average price: Modest
Area: Strand
Address: 56-59 Strand
London WC2N 5LR, UK
Phone: +44 20 7925 0050

#219
ASDA
Category: Grocery
Average price: Modest
Area: Charlton
Address: Bugsbys Way
London SE7 7ST, UK
Phone: +44 20 8858 3313

#220
Perform
Category: Kids Activities
Area: Highams Park
Address: Woodford Green Primary School
Sunset Avenue London IG8 0ST, UK
Phone: +44 845 400 4000

#221
LA Fitness
Category: Gym
Area: South Kensington
Address: 63-81 Pelham Street
London SW7 2NJ, UK
Phone: +44 20 7366 8080

#222
Laughing Halibut
Category: Fish & Chips
Area: Westminster
Address: 38 Strutton Ground
London SW1P 2HR, UK
Phone: +44 20 7799 2844

#223
Billy Elliot the Musical
Category: Performing Arts
Area: Covent Garden
Address: Victoria Street
London SW1H 0, UK
Phone: +44 7902 127654

#224
London Fields Park
Category: Park
Area: London Fields
Address: London Fields Westside
London E8 3EU, UK
Phone: +44 20 8356 8428

#225
Presto! Performing Arts
Category: Kids Activities
Area: Barking, Dagenham
Address: London IG11, UK
Phone: +44 7525 456736

#226
IWM London
Category: Museum
Area: Kennington
Address: Lambeth Road
London SE1 6HZ, UK
Phone: +44 20 7416 5000

#227
York Hall Leisure Centre
Category: Leisure Center
Area: Bethnal Green
Address: 5-15 Old Ford Rd
London E2 9PJ, UK
Phone: +44 20 8980 2243

#228
Golders Hill Park
Category: Park
Area: Hampstead Heath
Address: West Heath Avenue
London NW11 7QP, UK
Phone: +44 20 8455 5183

#229
The Castle Climbing Centre
Category: Climbing
Area: Harringay
Address: Green Lanes
London N4 2HA, UK
Phone: +44 20 8211 7000

#230
La Famiglia
Category: Italian, Gluten-Free
Average price: Expensive
Area: Chelsea
Address: 7 Langton Street
London SW10 0JL, UK
Phone: +44 20 7352 6095

#231
Primrose Hill
Category: Park
Area: Chalk Farm, Primrose Hill
Address: Primrose Hill Road
London NW3 3NA, UK
Phone: +44 20 7486 7905

#232
Poundland
Category: Discount Store
Average price: Inexpensive
Area: Alexandra Palace, Noel Park
Address: 51-53 High Road
London N22 6BH, UK
Phone: +44 20 8881 0133

#233
Perform
Category: Specialty School,
Kids Activities
Area: Blackheath
Address: St Michael and All Angels Churc 1
Pond Road London SE3 9JL, UK
Phone: +44 845 400 4000

#234
Ealing Common
Category: Park
Area: Ealing
Address: 23 Uxbridge Road
London W7 3XA, UK
Phone: +44 20 8992 2290

#235
Bouncy Castle UK
Category: Kids Activities
Area: Harrow & Wealdstone
Address: 6 Graham Road
London HA3 5RF, UK
Phone: +44 7940 224712

#236
Bobo Kids
Category: Baby Gear, Toy Store
Area: Chelsea
Address: 29 Elystan Street
London SW3 3NT, UK
Phone: +44 20 7838 1020

#237
Cheeky Monkeys
Category: Children's Clothing
Area: Clapham Park
Address: 104 Rodenhurst Road
London SW4 8AP, UK
Phone: +44 20 8623 9332

#238
Sports Xtra
Category: Kids Activities
Area: Barking, Dagenham
Address: London IG11, UK
Phone: +44 845 371 6121

#239
Kushti Kids
Category: Kids Activities
Area: Dagenham
Address: 545 Gale Street
London RM9 4TS, UK
Phone: +44 7957 339684

#240
Seahorse
Category: Fast Food, Fish & Chips
Area: Summerstown
Address: 446 Garratt Lane
London SW18 4HL, UK
Phone: +44 20 8947 7465

#241
Mohawk Spur Steak & Grill
Category: American
Average price: Modest
Area: Wandsworth
Address: Wandsworth High Street
London SW18 4JB, UK
Phone: +44 20 8874 0831

#242
Lloyds Lanes Ten Pin Bowling
Category: Bowling
Area: Raynes Park
Address: Bushey Road
London SW20 8DE, UK
Phone: +44 20 8544 9965

#243
Bank Of England Museum
Category: Museum, Art Gallery
Average price: Inexpensive
Area: The City
Address: Threadneedle Street
London EC2R 8AH, UK
Phone: +44 20 7601 5545

#244
Clissold Leisure Centre
Category: Leisure Center,
Swimming Pool
Area: Stoke Newington
Address: 63 Clissold Road
London N16 9EX, UK
Phone: +44 20 7254 5574

#245
Cafe Rouge
Category: Cafe
Average price: Modest
Area: Covent Garden, Strand
Address: 34 Wellington Street
London WC2E 9BT, UK
Phone: +44 20 7836 0998

#246
Cybercandy Covent Garden
Category: Candy Store
Average price: Expensive
Area: Covent Garden, Strand
Address: 3 Garrick Street
London WC2E 9BF, UK
Phone: +44 845 838 0958

#247
Virgin Active
Category: Gym
Area: Clerkenwell, Angel
Address: 333 Goswell Road
London EC1V 7DG, UK
Phone: +44 20 7014 9700

#248
Chix Chox
Category: Italian
Average price: Modest
Address: 793 High Road
London N12 8JT, UK
Phone: +44 20 8445 2016

#249
The Woman In Black
Category: Performing Arts
Area: Marylebone
Address: 30-31 Russell Street
London WC2B 5HH, UK
Phone: +44 20 7836 2238

#250
Regent's Park
Category: Park, Performing Arts
Area: Regent's Park
Address: The Storeyard Inner Circle
London NW1 4NR, UK
Phone: +44 20 7486 7905

#251
**The Paul Nicholas School
of Acting & Performing Arts**
Category: Dance School, Kids Activities
Area: West Wickham
Address: 142 High Street West Wickham
London BR4 0LZ, UK
Phone: +44 20 8462 9447

#252
The Foundling Museum
Category: Museum, Coffee & Tea
Area: Bloomsbury
Address: 40 Brunswick Square
London WC1N 1AZ, UK
Phone: +44 20 7841 3600

#253
Mona's Cafe
Category: Cafe
Average price: Inexpensive
Area: Marylebone
Address: 102 Crawford Street
London W1H 2HR, UK
Phone: +44 20 7724 7143

#254
Theatretrain
Category: Kids Activities
Area: Cheam
Address: Chatsworth Road
London SM3 8PW, UK
Phone: +44 20 8641 7419

#255
The Beach Hut
Category: Fish & Chips
Area: Highbury
Address: 28a Highbury Park
London N5 2AA, UK
Phone: +44 7939 852784

#256
Honey Jam
Category: Toy Store
Average price: Modest
Area: Notting Hill
Address: 2 Blenheim Crescent
London W11 1NN, UK
Phone: +44 20 7243 0449

#257
Elys
Category: Department Store
Average price: Expensive
Area: Wimbledon
Address: 16 St George's Road
London SW19 4DP, UK
Phone: +44 20 8946 9191

#258
Zizzi
Category: Pizza, Italian
Average price: Modest
Area: Chiswick
Address: 235 Chiswick High Road
London W4 4PU, UK
Phone: +44 20 8747 9400

#259
Perform
Category: Specialty School,
Kids Activities
Area: Beckenham
Address: St George's Church Hall
Albermarle Road London BR3 5HZ, UK
Phone: +44 845 400 4000

#260
National Geographic
Category: Cultural Center
Area: Piccadilly
Address: Regent Street
London W1B 4HT, UK
Phone: +44 20 7437 0144

#261
Soccer Scene
Category: Sporting Goods
Average price: Modest
Area: Fitzrovia
Address: 156 Oxford Street
London W1D 1ND, UK
Phone: +44 20 7436 6499

#262
Adams Childrenswear
Category: Children's Clothing,
Shoe Store
Area: Peckham
Address: 65 Rye Lane
London SE15 5EX, UK
Phone: +44 20 7277 9678

#263
Clissold Park
Category: Park
Area: Stoke Newington
Address: Green Lanes
London N4 2EY, UK
Phone: +44 20 8800 1021

#264
Kids Korner
Category: Kids Activities
Area: Epping Forest
Address: Epping New Road
London CM16 5HW, UK
Phone: +44 1992 813413

#265
Nomad Books
Category: Bookstore
Average price: Modest
Area: Fulham
Address: 781 Fulham Road
London SW6 5HA, UK
Phone: +44 20 7736 4000

#266
Nightingale
Category: British, Coffee & Tea,
Breakfast & Brunch
Average price: Inexpensive
Area: Balham
Address: 193 Balham High Road
London SW12 9BE, UK
Phone: +44 20 8673 7707

#267
Nando's
Category: Portuguese
Average price: Modest
Area: Fitzrovia
Address: 57-59 Goodge St
London W1T 1TH, UK
Phone: +44 20 7637 0708

#268
Super Camps
Category: Kids Activities
Area: Croydon
Address: Royal Russell School Coombe
Lane London CR9 5BX, UK
Phone: +44 1235 832222

#269
Ripley's Believe It Or Not!
Category: Museum
Area: Piccadilly
Address: 1 Piccadilly Circus
London W1J 0DA, UK
Phone: +44 20 3238 0022

#270
Bouncalot Castles
Category: Kids Activities
Area: Enfield
Address: London EN2 9DB, UK
Phone: +44 7815 054951

#271
1st Hainault Scout Group
Category: Kids Activities
Area: Hainault
Address: The Stockade Davids Way
London IG6 3BQ, UK
Phone: +44 20 8500 9992

#272
Brockwell Lido
Category: Swimming Pool, Gym, Yoga
Area: Streatham Hill
Address: Brockwell Park
London SE24 0PA, UK
Phone: +44 20 7274 3088

#273
Chi Combat System Bromley
Category: Martial Arts, Kids Activities
Area: Bromley
Address: London BR1 2TW, UK
Phone: +44 7826 517218

#274
Kidzology
Category: Kids Activities
Area: Hainault
Address: Unit 14 97 - 101 Peregrine Road
London IG6 3XJ, UK
Phone: +44 20 8501 2970

#275
Bromley bouncy castles
Category: Kids Activities
Area: Bromley
Address: Barham court
London BR2 8LA, UK
Phone: +44 7956 838687

#276
Kidzology
Category: Kids Activities
Area: Hainault
Address: Unit 14 97 - 101 Peregrine Road
London IG6 3XJ, UK
Phone: +44 20 8501 2970

#277
**Charlie Farley The All Round
Entertainer**
Category: Kids Activities
Area: Morden
Address: 309 Lower Morden Lane
London SM4 4NX, UK
Phone: +44 20 8395 7929

#278
Kings Hall
Category: Leisure Center,
Swimming Pool
Area: Hackney Downs
Address: 39 Lower Clapton Road
London E5 0NU, UK
Phone: +44 20 8985 2158

#279
Harrods
Category: Department Store
Average price: Exclusive
Area: Chelsea
Address: 135 Brompton Road
London SW1X 7XL, UK
Phone: +44 20 7730 1234

#280
Circus Circus
Category: Party & Event Planning,
Party Supplies
Area: Fulham
Address: 176 Wandsworth Bridge Rd
London SW6 2UQ, UK
Phone: +44 20 7731 4128

#281
Tartine et Chocolat
Category: Children's Clothing
Average price: Expensive
Area: Marylebone
Address: 66 South Molton Street
London W1K 5SX, UK
Phone: +44 4420 7629 7233

#282
At Your Fingertips
Category: Kids Activities, Nail Salon
Area: Chadwell Heath
Address: Chadwell Heath Romford Essex
London RM6 4NP, UK
Phone: +44 7896 604860

#283
Banner's
Category: Breakfast & Brunch
Average price: Modest
Area: Crouch End
Address: 21 Park Road
London N8 8TE, UK
Phone: +44 20 8348 2930

#284
Hala Restaurant
Category: Turkish
Average price: Inexpensive
Area: Noel Park, Turnpike Lane
Address: 29 Green Parade
London N4 1LG, UK
Phone: +44 20 8802 4883

#285
Davenports Magic Shop
Category: Toy Store, Hobby Shop
Area: Hayes, Strand
Address: 5-7 Charing Cross Underground
Arcade
London WC2N 4HZ, UK
Phone: +44 20 7836 0408

#286
Crocodile Antiques & Cafe
Category: Coffee & Tea, Antiques
Average price: Modest
Area: Muswell Hill
Address: 120-122 Muswell Hill Broadway
London N10 3RU, UK
Phone: +44 20 8444 0273

#287
Scotts Steak House
Category: British
Average price: Modest
Area: Soho
Address: 53 Shaftesbury Avenue
London W1D 6LB, UK
Phone: +44 20 7434 1935

#288
Golden Lane Swimming Pool
Category: Swimming Pool
Area: Barbican
Address: Fann Street
London EC1Y 0SH, UK
Phone: +44 20 7250 1464

#289
Susan Wainwright
Category: Gift Shop
Area: Hampstead Heath
Address: 31 South End Road
London NW3 2PY, UK
Phone: +44 20 7431 4337

#290
Early Learning Centre
Category: Toy Store
Area: Ealing
Address: The Broadway
London W5 5JY, UK
Phone: +44 20 8567 7076

#291
London RIB Voyages
Category: Boat Charters, Boating
Area: Southwark, Waterloo
Address: 39 York Road
London SE1 7NJ, UK
Phone: +44 20 7928 8933

#292
The London Bridge Experience
Category: Performing Arts
Area: London Bridge
Address: 2/4 Tooley Street
London SE1, UK
Phone: +44 845 301 0996

#293
Wicked
Category: Performing Arts
Area: Victoria
Address: 17 Wilton Road
London SW1V 1LG, UK
Phone: +44 844 826 8000

#294
Studio Six
Category: Spanish
Average price: Modest
Area: South Bank, Southwark
Address: 56 Upper Ground
London SE1 9PP, UK
Phone: +44 20 7928 6243

#295
National Portrait Gallery
Category: Art Gallery
Average price: Inexpensive
Area: Covent Garden, Strand
Address: St Martin's Place
London WC2H 0HE, UK
Phone: +44 20 7306 0055

#296
Queen Mothers Sports Centre
Category: Sports Club, Swimming Pool
Area: Victoria
Address: 223 Vauxhall Bridge Road
London SW1V 1EL, UK
Phone: +44 20 7630 5522

#297
Haggerston Park
Category: Park
Area: Haggerston
Address: 1 Queensbridge Road
London E2 8NP, UK
Phone: +44 20 7739 6288

#298
Virgin Active
Category: Gym, Swimming Pool
Address: 4-20 North Street
London SW4 0HG, UK
Phone: +44 20 7819 2555

#299
Mystical Fairies
Category: Party & Event Planning
Area: Hampstead Village
Address: 12 Flask Walk
London NW3 1HE, UK
Phone: +44 20 7431 1888

#300
London Eye
Category: Arts & Entertainment, Tours
Area: South Bank, Southwark
Address: Westminster Bridge Road
London SE1 7PB, UK
Phone: +44 870 500 0600

#301
Planet Hollywood
Category: American
Average price: Modest
Area: Leicester Square
Address: 57-60 Haymarket
London SW1Y 4QX, UK
Phone: +44 20 7287 1000

#302
Byron
Category: Burgers
Average price: Modest
Area: Finchley Road, Swiss Cottage
Address: 255 Finchley Road
London NW3 6LU, UK
Phone: +44 20 7794 3323

#303
Pho
Category: Vietnamese
Average price: Modest
Area: Aldgate
Address: 48 Brushfield Street
London E1 6AG, UK
Phone: +44 20 7377 6436

#304
Rascals Theatre School
Category: Kids Activities
Area: Chadwell Heath, Dagenham
Address: Warren Comp School Whalebone
Lane North London RM6 6SB, UK
Phone: +44 1376 331543

#305
Rosa's Westfield Stratford
Category: Thai
Average price: Modest
Area: Stratford
Address: World Food Court
London E15 1AA, UK
Phone: +44 20 8519 1302

#306
Ragged School Museum
Category: Museum
Area: Mile End (South)
Address: 46-50 Copperfield Road
London E3 4RR, UK
Phone: +44 20 8980 6405

#307
JD Sports
Category: Sporting Goods
Area: Stratford
Address: 79-80 The Mall
London E15 1XQ, UK
Phone: +44 20 8534 9869

#308
TGI Fridays Covent Garden
Category: American
Average price: Modest
Area: Covent Garden, Strand
Address: 6 Bedford Street
London WC2E 9HZ, UK
Phone: +44 20 7379 0585

#309
Kentish Town City Farm
Category: Zoo
Area: Parliament Hill/Dartmouth Park
Address: 1 Cressfield Close
London NW5 4BN, UK
Phone: +44 20 7916 5421

#310
Pizza Express
Category: Pizza, Italian
Area: Bloomsbury
Address: 114-117 Southampton Row
London WC1B 5AA, UK
Phone: +44 20 7430 1011

#311
BJ's Bouncy Castles Hire
Category: Kids Activities
Area: Addington
Address: Milne park
London CR0, UK
Phone: +44 7956 838687

#312
London Wall Bar and Kitchen
Category: British, Pub
Average price: Modest
Area: Barbican
Address: 150 London Wall
London EC2Y 5HN, UK
Phone: +44 20 7600 7340

#313
Priceless Shoes
Category: Shoe Store
Area: East Ham
Address: 87 High Street N
London E6 1HZ, UK
Phone: +44 1274 628227

#314
Fratelli La Bufala
Category: Italian
Average price: Expensive
Area: Leicester Square
Address: 40 Shaftesbury Avenue
London W1D 7EY, UK
Phone: +44 20 7734 3404

#315
Odeon Wimbledon
Category: Cinema
Area: Wimbledon
Address: 31-37 The Broadway
London SW19 1QG, UK
Phone: +44 871 224 4007

#316
The Old Operating Theatre
Category: Museum, Art Gallery
Average price: Inexpensive
Area: London Bridge
Address: 9a St Thomas St
London SE1 9RY, UK
Phone: +44 20 7188 2679

#317
Flame Restaurant
Category: Indian
Area: Harringay, West Green
Address: 551 Green Lanes
London N8 0RL, UK
Phone: +44 20 8340 9691

#318
Little Ilford Park
Category: Park, Tennis
Area: East Ham
Address: Church Road
London E12 6HB, UK
Phone: +44 20 8552 0939

#319
Kidspace Romford
Category: Kids Activities
Area: Romford
Address: Unit 1D The Brewery
London RM1 1AU, UK
Phone: +44 1708 768003

#320
Decathlon UK
Category: Sporting Goods
Average price: Modest
Area: Bermondsey, Canada Water
Address: Surrey Quays Road
London SE16 2XU, UK
Phone: +44 20 7394 2000

#321
Syon Park
Category: Park
Area: Brentford
Address: Syon Park
London TW8 8JF, UK
Phone: +44 20 8560 0882

#322
The Gloucester
Category: British
Average price: Modest
Area: Belgravia
Address: 187 Sloane Street
London SW1X 9QR, UK
Phone: +44 20 7235 0298

#323
The Primrose Eatery
Category: American, Pizza
Average price: Modest
Area: Chalk Farm, Primrose Hill
Address: 38 Primrose Hill Road
London NW3 3AD, UK
Phone: +44 20 7483 3222

#324
La Porchetta
Category: Italian, Pizza
Average price: Inexpensive
Area: Muswell Hill
Address: 43 Muswell Hill Broadway
London N10 1DE, UK
Phone: +44 20 8883 1500

#325
The British Museum
Category: Museum
Area: Bloomsbury
Address: Great Russell Street
London WC1B 3DG, UK
Phone: +44 20 7323 8299

#326
Oscars Den
Category: Party Supplies, Costumes
Average price: Modest
Area: West Hampstead
Address: 127-129 Abbey Road
London NW6 4SL, UK
Phone: +44 20 7328 6683

#327
Sacro Cuore
Category: Pizza, Italian
Average price: Modest
Area: Kensal Rise, Queen's Park
Address: 45 Chamberlayne Road
London NW10 3NB, UK
Phone: +44 20 8960 8558

#328
Burgess Park
Category: Park, Fishing
Area: Burgess Park
Address: Albany Road
London SE5 0RJ, UK
Phone: +44 20 7703 3911

#329
Serpentine Gallery Bookshop
Category: Bookstore, Art Gallery
Average price: Modest
Area: Hyde Park, Kensington
Address: Kensington Gardens
London W2 3XA, UK
Phone: +44 20 7706 4907

#330
Kidspace
Category: Kids Activities
Area: Purley
Address: 619 Purley Way
London CR0 4RJ, UK
Phone: +44 20 8686 0040

#331
Spaghetti House
Category: Italian, Pizza
Average price: Modest
Area: Covent Garden, Strand
Address: 30 St Martins Lane
London WC2N 4ER, UK
Phone: +44 20 7836 1626

#332
Museum of London Docklands
Category: Museum, Art Gallery
Average price: Inexpensive
Area: Canary Wharf, Isle of Dogs, Poplar
Address: West India Quay
London E14 4AL, UK
Phone: +44 20 7001 9844

#333
McDonald's Restaurant
Category: American, Fast Food
Average price: Inexpensive
Area: Upton Park, Wanstead
Address: 322-324 Romford Road
London E7 8BD, UK
Phone: +44 20 8519 3535

#334
BJ's Bouncy Castles
Category: Kids Activities
Area: Orpington
Address: 1 Small Civic Hall
London BR6 8PR, UK
Phone: +44 7956 838687

#335
Camley Street Natural Park
Category: Park
Area: King's Cross
Address: 12 Camley St
London NW1 0PW, UK
Phone: +44 20 7833 2311

#336
South Park
Category: Park
Area: Fulham
Address: 88 Peterborough Rd
London SW6 3HH, UK
Phone: +44 20 7731 8989

#337
Idea Store Whitechapel
Category: Library, Education
Area: Whitechapel
Address: 321 Whitechapel Rd
London E1 1BU, UK
Phone: +44 20 7364 4332

#338
Everyman Baker Street
Category: Cinema
Area: Marylebone
Address: 96-98 Baker Street
London W1U 6TJ, UK
Phone: +44 871 906 9060

#339
Electric Cinema
Category: Cinema
Area: Notting Hill
Address: 191 Portobello Road
London W11 2ED, UK
Phone: +44 20 7908 9696

#340
Victoria and Albert Museum
Category: Museum
Area: Knightsbridge
Address: Cromwell Road
London SW7 2RL, UK
Phone: +44 20 7942 2000

#341
Putney Library
Category: Library
Area: Wandsworth
Address: 1 Disraeli Road
London SW15 2DR, UK
Phone: +44 20 8871 7090

#342
Electric Cinema
Category: Cinema
Area: Notting Hill
Address: 191 Portobello Road
London W11 2ED, UK
Phone: +44 20 7908 9696

#343
Hollywood Bowl
Category: Bowling
Area: Bermondsey, Canada Water,
Rotherhithe, Surrey Quays
Address: 3a Teredo Street
London SE16 7LW, UK
Phone: +44 844 826 1470

#344
Kelsey Park
Category: Park
Area: Eden Park
Address: 348 Manor Way
Bromley BR3 3LH, UK
Phone: +44 20 8313 4471

#345
Gourmet Burger Kitchen
Category: Burgers
Average price: Modest
Area: Greenwich
Address: 45 Greenwich Church Street
London SE10 9BL, UK
Phone: +44 20 8858 3920

#346
Dulwich Riding Scool
Category: Horseback Riding
Area: Dulwich, West Dulwich
Address: Dulwich Common
London SE21 7EX, UK
Phone: +44 20 8693 2944

#347
Three Potato Four
Category: Children's Clothing,
Baby Gear & Furniture, Toy Store
Average price: Modest
Area: Newington Green
Address: 44-45 Newington Green
London N16 9QH, UK
Phone: +44 20 7704 2228

#348
BJ's Bouncy Castles
Category: Kids Activities
Area: Orpington
Address: York Rise
London BR6 8PR, UK
Phone: +44 1959 702007

#349
Jumpabouts
Category: Kids Activities
Area: North Cray
Address: cocksure lane
London DA14 5EY, UK
Phone: +44 20 8300 5458

#350
Frizzante
Category: Mediterranean
Average price: Modest
Area: Haggerston
Address: 1a Goldsmiths Row
London E2 8QA, UK
Phone: +44 20 7739 2266

#351
Jamie's Italian
Category: Italian
Average price: Modest
Area: Clerkenwell, Angel
Address: 403 St John Street
London EC1V 4PL, UK
Phone: +44 20 3435 9915

#352
Green Baby
Category: Children's Clothing
Average price: Modest
Area: Notting Hill
Address: 5 Elgin Crescent
London W11 2JA, UK
Phone: +44 20 7792 8140

#353
Laville Café
Category: Italian, French
Average price: Modest
Area: Little Venice, Paddington
Address: 453 Edgware Road
London W2 1TH, UK
Phone: +44 20 7706 2620

#354
Canada Water Library
Category: Library
Area: Bermondsey, Canada Water
Address: 21 Surrey Quays Road
London SE16 7AR, UK
Phone: +44 20 7527 2000

#355
Tumble Tots
Category: Kids Activities
Area: Uxbridge
Address: 25 Hercies Road
London UB10, UK
Phone: +44 1483 851035

#356
Abu Zaad
Category: Middle Eastern
Average price: Modest
Area: Marylebone
Address: 128 Edgware Rd
London W2 2DZ, UK
Phone: +44 20 7262 8304

#357
Jigsaw
Category: Women's Clothing,
Men's Clothing, Children's Clothing
Average price: Modest
Area: Notting Hill
Address: 190-192 Westbourne Grove
London W11 2RH, UK
Phone: +44 20 7727 0322

#358
Serpentine Lido
Category: Swimming Pool
Area: Hyde Park, Kensington
Address: Serpentine South Side
Hyde Park W2 2UH, UK
Phone: +44 20 7706 3422

#359
Stingray Cafe
Category: Mediterranean
Average price: Inexpensive
Area: Kentish Town
Address: 135a-135d Fortess Road
London NW5 2HR, UK
Phone: +44 20 7482 4855

#360
Esporta Health & Fitness Club
Category: Gym
Area: Finchley Road, Swiss Cottage
Address: 02 Centre Finchley Road
London NW3 6LU, UK
Phone: +44 20 7644 2400

#361
Drum Jam
Category: Performing Arts
Area: Euston, Camden Town
Address: 89 Plender Street
London NW1 1TR, UK
Phone: +44 20 8346 7513

#362
Cheeky Monkeys
Category: Toy Store
Area: Notting Hill
Address: 202 Kensington Pk Road
London W11 1NR, UK
Phone: +44 20 7313 4634

#363
Queens
Category: Skating Rinks, Bowling
Area: Bayswater
Address: 17 Queensway
London W2 4QP, UK
Phone: +44 20 7229 0172

#364
Russia Dock Woodland
Category: Park
Area: Bermondsey, Canada Water,
Rotherhithe
Address: Salter Road
London SE16 6QN, UK
Phone: +44 20 7237 7586

#365
Drum Jam
Category: Performing Arts
Area: Euston, Camden Town
Address: 89 Plender Street
London NW1 1TR, UK
Phone: +44 20 8346 7513

#366
Tower Of London
Category: Museum, Landmark
Area: Aldgate, The City
Address: The Tower of London
London EC3N 4AB, UK
Phone: +44 844 482 7777

#367
LEGO
Category: Toy Store
Average price: Expensive
Area: Shepherd's Bush, White City
Address: Ariel Way London W12 7GF
Phone: +44 20 8749 1059

#368
Petrie Museum of Archaeology
Category: Museum
Area: Bloomsbury
Address: Gower Street
London WC1E 6BT, UK
Phone: +44 20 7679 2000

#369
Le Pain Quotidien
Category: French, Bakery
Average price: Modest
Area: Covent Garden, Strand
Address: 48 & 49 the Market
London WC2E 8RF, UK
Phone: +44 20 3657 6928

#370
Hammersmith Park
Category: Park
Area: Shepherd's Bush, White City
Address: South Africa Road
London W12 7PA, UK
Phone: +44 20 8753 4103

#371
The Portman
Category: Breakfast & Brunch
Average price: Expensive
Area: Marylebone
Address: 51 Upper Berkeley Street
London W1H 7QW, UK
Phone: +44 20 7723 8996

#372
Wagamama
Category: Japanese, Asian Fusion
Average price: Modest
Area: Shepherd's Bush, White City
Address: Ariel Way
London W12 7SL, UK
Phone: +44 20 8749 9073

#373
34
Category: American
Average price: Exclusive
Area: Marylebone
Address: 34 Grovesnor Square
London W1K 2HD, UK
Phone: +44 20 3350 3434

#374
Tooting Common
Category: Park
Area: Tooting, Tooting Bec
Address: Tooting Bec Road
London SW16 1RT, UK
Phone: +44 20 8871 6347

#375
Toy Stop
Category: Toy Store
Area: Putney
Address: Putney High Street
London SW15 1TW, UK
Phone: +44 20 8788 5180

#376
Cyclopolis Bicycle Shop & Repair Service
Category: Bikes, Active Life
Average price: Modest
Area: Balham
Address: 54 Balham High Road
London SW12 9AQ, UK
Phone: +44 20 8673 7153

#377
Toys 'R' Us
Category: Toy Store
Area: Waddon
Address: Purley Way
London CR0 4XL, UK
Phone: +44 20 8686 3133

#378
Hollywood Bowl
Category: Bowling
Area: North Finchley
Address: Great North Leisure Park
London N12 0GL, UK
Phone: +44 20 8446 6667

#379
Towpath Café
Category: Mediterranean,
Modern European, Coffee & Tea
Average price: Modest
Area: De Beauvoir
Address: 42 De Beauvoir Crescent
London N1 5SB, UK
Phone: +44 20 7254 7606

#380
Strada
Category: Italian
Average price: Modest
Area: Clerkenwell
Address: 8-10 Exmouth Market
London EC1R 4QA, UK
Phone: +44 20 7278 0800

#381
Polka Theatre
Category: Performing Arts,
Music Venues
Area: Wimbledon
Address: 240 The Broadway
London SW19 1SB, UK
Phone: +44 20 8543 4888

#382
Crystal Palace Park
Category: Park
Area: Crystal Palace, South Norwood
Address: Anerley Hill
London SE19 2BA, UK
Phone: +44 20 8778 9496

#383
The Monument
Category: Landmark, Historical Building
Area: Aldgate
Address: Monument Street
London EC3R 8AH, UK
Phone: +44 20 7626 2717

#384
Charlie & The Chocolate Factory
Category: Performing Arts
Area: Covent Garden, Strand
Address: Theatre Royal Drury Lane
London WC2B 5JF, UK
Phone: +44 844 858 8877

#385
Carnaby Burger Co
Category: Burgers
Average price: Modest
Area: Soho
Address: 4 Newburgh Street
London W1F 7RF, UK
Phone: +44 20 7287 6983

#386
Portobello Ristorante Pizzeria
Category: Italian, Pizza
Average price: Modest
Area: Notting Hill
Address: 7 Ladbroke Road
London W11 3PA, UK
Phone: +44 20 7221 1373

#387
The Holiday Club and After School Club - West Drayton
Category: Kids Activities
Area: Hillingdon, West Drayton
Address: Kingston Lane
London UB7 9EA, UK
Phone: +44 7828 184316

#388
New Winner
Category: Chinese, Thai
Average price: Inexpensive
Area: Lewisham
Address: 278 Lewisham High St
London SE13 6JZ, UK
Phone: +44 20 8690 7614

#389
Hunterian Museum
Category: Museum
Area: Holborn
Address: 35-43 Lincoln's Inn Fields
London WC2A 3PE, UK
Phone: +44 20 7869 6560

#390
The London Particular
Category: Cafe
Average price: Modest
Area: New Cross
Address: 399 New Cross Road
London SE14 6LA, UK
Phone: +44 20 8692 6149

#391
Odeon
Category: Cinema
Area: Muswell Hill
Address: Fortis Green Road
London N10 3HP, UK
Phone: +44 871 224 4007

#392
West 1 Climbing Wall
Category: Climbing
Area: Marylebone
Address: Seymour place
London W1H 5TJ, UK
Phone: +44 845 363 1177

#393
Ciros Pizza Pomodoro
Category: Pizza, Italian
Area: Chelsea
Address: 51 Beauchamp Place
London SW3 1NY, UK
Phone: +44 20 7589 1278

#394
Arancina
Category: Pizza, Italian, Fast Food
Average price: Modest
Area: Bayswater
Address: 19 Westbourne Grove
London W2 4UA, UK
Phone: +44 20 7792 9777

#395
Covent Garden Market
Category: Arts & Crafts, Landmark &
Historical Building, Farmers Market
Average price: Modest
Area: Covent Garden
Address: London WC2E 8RF, UK
Phone: +44 870 780 5001

#396
PeckhamPlex
Category: Cinema
Area: Peckham
Address: 95a Rye Lane
London SE15 4ST, UK
Phone: +44 870 042 9399

#397
Oliver Bonas
Category: Women's Clothing, Jewelry, Cards
& Stationery, Home Decor
Area: Clapham
Address: 23 The Pavement
London SW4 0JA, UK
Phone: +44 20 7720 8272

#398
Snakes and Ladders
Category: Playground
Area: Brentford
Address: Syon Park
Richmond TW8 8JF, UK
Phone: +44 20 8847 0946

#399
Standard Fish Bar
Category: Fish & Chips
Average price: Inexpensive
Area: Greenwich
Address: 26 Old Dover Road
London SE3 7BT, UK
Phone: +44 20 8858 0207

#400
The Royal Forest
Category: British, Pub
Area: Chingford
Address: 4 Rangers Road
London E4 7QH, UK
Phone: +44 20 8523 7246

#401
Piccolo Caffe
Category: Cafe, Juice Bar
Area: Chiswick
Address: Duke Rd
London W4 2DF, UK
Phone: +44 7525 773659

#402
The Arsenal Museum
Category: Soccer, Museum
Area: Arsenal, Lower Holloway
Address: 75 Drayton Park
London N5 1BU, UK
Phone: +44 20 7704 4504

#403
Waitrose
Category: Grocery
Average price: Modest
Area: Chelsea
Address: 196-198 Kings Road
London SW3 5XP, UK
Phone: +44 20 7351 2775

#404
Aquaterra Leisure
Category: Leisure Center
Area: Holloway, Lower Holloway
Address: Hornsey Rd
London N7 7NY, UK
Phone: +44 20 7686 8811

#405
Cannons Health Club
Category: Gym
Area: Southfields
Address: Burr Road
London SW18 4SQ, UK
Phone: +44 870 121 0999

#406
Ed's Easy Diner - Mayfair
Category: American, Burgers
Average price: Expensive
Area: Marylebone
Address: 14 Woodstock Street
London W1C, UK
Phone: +44 20 7493 9916

#407
Rodwins
Category: Arts & Crafts
Average price: Inexpensive
Area: Southgate
Address: 92 Crown Lane
London N14 5EN, UK
Phone: +44 20 8886 7273

#408
Chimichanga
Category: Mexican
Average price: Modest
Area: South Woodford
Address: 190 George Lane
London E18 1AY, UK
Phone: +44 20 8989 5356

#409
Jamie's Italian
Category: Italian
Average price: Modest
Area: Isle of Dogs, West India Docks
Address: 2 Churchill Place
London E14 5RB, UK
Phone: +44 20 3002 5252

#410
Virgin Active
Category: Gym
Area: Finchley Road, Swiss Cottage
Address: 255 Finchley Road
London NW3 6LU, UK
Phone: +44 20 7644 2400

#411
The Holiday Club and After School Club - St. Andrews
Category: Kids Activities
Area: Uxbridge
Address: Hermitage Primary School Belmont Rd, London UB8 1RB, UK
Phone: +44 7859 002363

#412
Caramel
Category: Baby Gear & Furniture, Children's Clothing
Average price: Expensive
Area: Notting Hill
Address: 77 Ledbury Rd
London W11 2AG, UK
Phone: +44 20 7727 0906

#413
Thai Taste
Category: Thai
Average price: Expensive
Area: South Kensington
Address: 130 Cromwell Road
London SW7 4ET, UK
Phone: +44 20 7373 1647

#414
Pizza Metro Pizza
Category: Pizza
Average price: Modest
Area: Clapham, Clapham Common
Address: 64 Battersea Rise
London SW11 1EQ, UK
Phone: +44 20 7228 3812

#415
The Parlour
Category: Ice Cream, American
Average price: Expensive
Area: Piccadilly
Address: 181 Piccadilly
London W1A 1ER, UK
Phone: +44 20 7734 8040

#416
Virgin Active
Category: Gym
Area: Summerstown
Address: 1 Merantum Way
London SW19, UK
Phone: +44 20 8495 8500

#417
Hyde Park Stables
Category: Horseback Riding
Area: Paddington
Address: 63 Bathurst Mews
London W2 2SB, UK
Phone: +44 20 7723 2813

#418
The Garden Café
Category: British, Tea Room, Cafe
Average price: Modest
Area: Regent's Park
Address: Inner Circle
London NW1 4NU, UK
Phone: +44 20 7935 5729

#419
Stave Hill Ecological Park
Category: Park, Local Flavor
Area: Bermondsey, Canada Water
Address: Timber Pond Road
London SE16 6AX, UK
Phone: +44 20 7237 9175

#420
Surrey Quays Shopping Centre
Category: Shopping Center
Average price: Modest
Area: Bermondsey, Canada Water, Rotherhithe, Surrey Quays
Address: 43 Surrey Quays Shopping Centre
London SE16 7LL, UK
Phone: +44 20 7237 5282

#421
Wildwood
Category: Italian
Average price: Modest
Area: South Kensington
Address: 154-156 Gloucester Rd
London SW7 4TD, UK
Phone: +44 20 7370 0070

#422
Westway Sports Centre
Category: Climbing
Area: North Kensington
Address: 1 Crowthorne Road
London W10 6RP, UK
Phone: +44 20 8969 0992

#423
Tate Modern
Category: Museum
Area: South Bank, Southwark
Address: Bankside
London SE1 9JE, UK
Phone: +44 20 7887 8888

#424
Giraffe
Category: Breakfast & Brunch
Average price: Modest
Area: Spitalfields
Address: 1 Crispin Place
London E1 6DW, UK
Phone: +44 20 3116 2000

#425
Owl Bookshop
Category: Bookstore
Average price: Modest
Area: Camden Town
Address: 209 Kentish Town Road
London NW5 2JU, UK
Phone: +44 20 7485 7793

#426
N20 Restaurant
Category: British
Area: Totteridge, Whetstone
Address: 1105-111 High Road
London N20 0PT, UK
Phone: +44 20 8445 5795

#427
Namco Station
Category: Landmark, Historical Building
Area: Southwark, Waterloo
Address: Westminster Bridge Road
London SE1, UK
Phone: +44 20 7967 1066

#428
Parents Paradise
Category: Kids Activities
Area: Bushey
Address: Unit C Greatham Rd Watford
WD23 2NZ, UK
Phone: +44 1923 248747

#429
Centonove
Category: Italian
Area: Notting Hill
Address: 109 Westbourne Park Road
London W2 5QL, UK
Phone: +44 20 7221 1746

#430
The Scoop at More London
Category: Performing Arts,
Music Venues
Average price: Inexpensive
Area: London Bridge
Address: 2A More London Riverside
London SE1 2DB, UK
Phone: +44 20 7403 4866

#431
**The Holiday Club and After School
Club - Whitehall**
Category: Kids Activities
Area: Hillingdon
Address: Cowley Road
London UB8 2LX, UK
Phone: +44 7813 657366

#432
Pollyanna
Category: Children's Clothing,
Shoe Store
Average price: Expensive
Area: Fulham, Parsons Green
Address: 811 Fulham Road
London SW6 5HG, UK
Phone: +44 20 7731 0673

#433
Trocadero London
Category: Amusement Park
Area: Soho
Address: 1 Warwick Street
London W1B 5LR, UK
Phone: +44 20 7287 9216

#434
Castle Kingdom
Category: Kids Activities
Area: Hillingdon, West Drayton
Address: west drayton
London UB7 7AW, UK
Phone: +44 1895 811018

#435
The Brewery Shopping Centre
Category: Shopping Center
Average price: Expensive
Area: Romford
Address: Waterloo Road
London RM1 1AU, UK
Phone: +44 1708 748157

#436
The Entertainer
Category: Toy Store
Average price: Modest
Area: Wimbledon
Address: 7 The Broadway
London SW19 1PS, UK
Phone: +44 844 800 5133

#437
Seymour Leisure Centre
Category: Leisure Center
Area: Marylebone
Address: Seymour Place
London W1H 5TJ, UK
Phone: +44 20 7723 8019

#438
Lyndons Art & Graphics
Category: Arts & Crafts
Average price: Exclusive
Area: Notting Hill
Address: Unit 1 216 Kensington Park Road,
London W11 1NR, UK
Phone: +44 20 7727 5192

#439
Pizza East
Category: Pizza, Italian
Average price: Modest
Area: Kensal Town
Address: 310 Portobello Road
London W10 5TA, UK
Phone: +44 20 8969 4500

#440
Pied Piper
Category: Shoe Store
Area: Putney
Address: 234 Upper Richmond Road
London SW15 6TG, UK
Phone: +44 20 8788 1635

#441
La Dolce Vita
Category: Italian
Average price: Modest
Area: Kennington
Address: 4-5 London Road
London SE1 6JZ, UK
Phone: +44 20 7928 7138

#442
George's Portobello Fish Bar
Category: Fish & Chips
Average price: Modest
Area: Kensal Town
Address: 329 Portobello Road
London W10 5SA, UK
Phone: +44 20 8969 7895

#443
Wavelengths Leisure Pool
Category: Swimming Pool,
Leisure Center
Area: Deptford
Address: Giffin Street
London SE8 4RJ, UK
Phone: +44 20 8694 1134

#444
Good Vibes Covent Garden
Category: Sports Club, Yoga
Area: Covent Garden
Address: 14-16 Betterton Street
London WC2H 9BU, UK
Phone: +44 20 7240 6111

#445
Bruce Castle Museum
Category: Museum
Area: Tottenham
Address: Lordship Lane
London N17 8NU, UK
Phone: +44 20 8808 8772

#446
Kitchen & Pantry
Category: Coffee & Tea, Tea Room
Average price: Modest
Area: Chiswick
Address: 216-218 Chiswick High Road
London W4, UK
Phone: +44 20 8747 0006

#447
Fagins Toys
Category: Toy Store
Average price: Modest
Area: Muswell Hill
Address: 84 Fortis Green Rd
London N10 3HN, UK
Phone: +44 20 8444 0282

#448
Leyton Leisure Lagoon
Category: Leisure Center,
Swimming Pool
Area: Leyton
Address: 763 High Road Leyton
London E10 5AB, UK
Phone: +44 20 8558 8858

#449
Oasis Sports Centre
Category: Leisure Center, Sports Club
Area: Covent Garden
Address: 32 Endell Street
London WC2H 9AG, UK
Phone: +44 20 7831 1804

#450
The Third Space
Category: Gym
Area: Soho
Address: 13 Sherwood Street
London W1F 7BR, UK
Phone: +44 20 7439 6333

#451
Pizza Express
Category: Pizza, Italian
Average price: Modest
Area: Aldgate
Address: 232-283 BiShopgate
London EC2M 4QD, UK
Phone: +44 20 7247 2838

#452
Buona Sera Jam
Category: Italian
Average price: Expensive
Area: Chelsea
Address: 289a Kings Rd
London SW3 5EW, UK
Phone: +44 20 7352 8827

#453
David & Goliath
Category: Children's Clothing,
Women's Clothing, Accessories
Average price: Expensive
Area: Covent Garden
Address: 4 Covent Garden
London WC2E 8HB, UK
Phone: +44 20 7240 3640

#454
Burger King
Category: American, Fast Food
Area: Stratford
Address: K1 Great Eastern Road
London E15 1BB, UK
Phone: +44 20 8536 0100

#455
Vue
Category: Cinema
Area: Ealing
Address: Kendal Avenue
London W3 0PA, UK
Phone: +44 871 224 0240

#456
Blue Lagoon
Category: Thai
Average price: Modest
Area: Holland Park
Address: 286 Kensington High Street
London W14 8NZ, UK
Phone: +44 20 7603 1231

#457
Mega City Comics
Category: Comic Books, Bookstore
Average price: Modest
Area: Camden Town
Address: 18 Inverness Street
London NW1 7HJ, UK
Phone: +44 20 7485 9320

#458
Rockboard Scooter UK
Category: Bike Rentals
Area: Farringdon
Address: Unit 36 88-90
London EC1N 8PN, UK
Phone: +44 844 811 6094

#459
Toys 'R' Us
Category: Toy Store, Hobby Shop
Average price: Expensive
Area: Peckham
Address: 760 Old Kent Road
London SE15 1NJ, UK
Phone: +44 20 7732 7322

#460
Canta Napoli
Category: Italian, Pizza
Average price: Modest
Area: Chiswick
Address: 9A Devonshire Road
London W4 2EU, UK
Phone: +44 20 8994 5225

#461
Bushy Park
Category: Park
Area: Teddington
Address: London KT1 4BA, UK
Phone: +44 20 8979 1586

#462
Bistro Union
Category: British
Average price: Modest
Area: Clapham Park
Address: 40 Abbeville Road
London SW4 9NG, UK
Phone: +44 20 7042 6400

#463
Belgo Centraal
Category: Belgian
Average price: Modest
Area: Covent Garden
Address: 50 Earlham Street
London WC2H 9LJ, UK
Phone: +44 20 7813 2233

#464
Painted Earth
Category: Arcade, Arts & Crafts
Area: Camden Town
Address: The Stables Market The Stables
Mkt Chalk Far M Road
London NW1 8AH, UK
Phone: +44 20 7424 8983

#465
Janet Adegoke Swimming Pool
Category: Swimming Pool
Area: Acton, Shepherd's Bush
Address: Bloemfontein Road
London W12 7DB, UK
Phone: +44 20 8735 4900

#466
Nando's
Category: Portuguese, Chicken Wings
Average price: Inexpensive
Area: Greenwich
Address: Millennium Way
London SE10 0AX, UK
Phone: +44 20 8269 2401

#467
Painted Earth
Category: Arcade, Arts & Crafts
Area: Camden Town
Address: The Stables Market The Stables
Mkt Chalk Far M Road
London NW1 8AH, UK
Phone: +44 20 7424 8983

#468
Camden Town Library
Category: Library
Area: Euston, Camden Town
Address: 218 Eversholt Street
London NW1 1BD, UK
Phone: +44 20 7911 1563

#469
Leon
Category: Fast Food, Mediterranean
Average price: Modest
Area: Blackfriars
Address: 12 Ludgate Circus
London EC4M 7LQ, UK
Phone: +44 20 7489 1580

#470
Giraffe
Category: Breakfast & Brunch
Average price: Modest
Area: Belsize Park
Address: 196-198 Haverstock Hill
London NW3 2AG, UK
Phone: +44 20 7431 3812

#471
Nando's
Category: Portuguese, Chicken Wings
Average price: Expensive
Area: Chiswick
Address: 187-189 Chiswick High Rd
London W4 2DR, UK
Phone: +44 20 8995 7533

#472
Forbidden Planet
Category: Bookstore, Comic Books
Average price: Modest
Area: Covent Garden
Address: 179 Shaftesbury Avenue London
WC2H 8JR, UK
Phone: +44 20 7420 3666

#473
Happy Returns
Category: Toy Store
Area: Belsize Park, Hampstead Village
Address: 36 Rosslyn Hill
London NW3 1NH, UK
Phone: +44 20 7435 2431

#474
Virgin Active
Category: Gym
Area: Ealing
Address: Ealing Broadway Centre
London W5 5JY, UK
Phone: +44 20 8579 9433

#475
The Greenwich Union
Category: Pub, Restaurant
Average price: Modest
Area: Greenwich
Address: 56 Royal Hill
London SE10 8RT, UK
Phone: +44 20 8692 6258

#476
Lammas Park Play Centre
Category: Park
Address: Elers Road
London W13 9QD, UK
Phone: +44 20 8810 0240

#477
Lucas Gardens
Category: Park
Area: Camberwell
Address: Peckham Rd
London SE5 8PX, UK
Phone: +44 20 7525 6433

#478
One Small Step One Giant Leap
Category: Shoe Store
Area: Roehampton
Address: 409 Upper Richmond Rd
West London SW14 7NX, UK
Phone: +44 20 8487 1288

#479
The Disney Store
Category: Toy Store, Children's Clothing
Average price: Expensive
Area: Croydon
Address: 9899 Whitgift Centre
London CR0 1US, UK
Phone: +44 20 8649 9349

#480
Camden Arts Centre
Category: Performing Arts, Art Gallery
Average price: Inexpensive
Area: Finchley Road, Swiss Cottage
Address: Arkwright Road
London NW3 6DG, UK
Phone: +44 20 7472 5500

#481
Zen Cafe
Category: Cafe
Area: South Bank, Southwark
Address: Riverside Building
London SE1 7PB, UK
Phone: +44 20 7928 5047

#482
Peacock's Store
Category: Department Store,
Discount Store, Children's Clothing
Area: Dalston
Address: Kingsland High Street
London E8 2PA, UK
Phone: +44 20 7923 4363

#483
Carry Me Home
Category: Children's Clothing,
Baby Gear & Furniture
Average price: Modest
Area: Soho
Address: Unit 2 9 Kingly Court
London W1B 5PW, UK
Phone: +44 20 7434 1840

#484
Victoria Palace Theatre
Category: Performing Arts
Area: Westminster
Address: Victoria Street
London SW1E 5LA, UK
Phone: +44 844 248 5000

#485
The Works
Category: Bookstore
Average price: Inexpensive
Area: Croydon
Address: 9 Whitgift Centre
London CR0 1UP, UK
Phone: +44 20 8760 0683

#486
Fitness First Platinum
Category: Gym
Area: Liverpool Street / Broadgate
Address: Unit 12
London EC2M 7QA, UK
Phone: +44 844 571 2895

#487
The Ritzy
Category: Cinema
Area: Brixton
Address: Brixton Oval
London SW2 1JG, UK
Phone: +44 20 7733 2229

#488
Alexandra Recreation Ground
Category: Soccer, Playground
Area: Sydenham
Address: Alexandra Road
London SE26, UK
Phone: +44 20 8313 4493

#489
Tarantella
Category: Italian
Average price: Modest
Area: Chiswick
Address: 4 Elliott Road
London W4 1PE, UK
Phone: +44 20 8987 8877

#490
Alexandra Palace
Category: Music Venues, Market
Average price: Modest
Area: Alexandra Palace, Wood Green
Address: Alexandra Palace Way
London N22 7AY, UK
Phone: +44 20 8365 2121

#491
Clink Prison Museum
Category: Art Gallery, Museum
Average price: Inexpensive
Area: London Bridge, South Bank
Address: 1 Clink St
London SE1 9DG, UK
Phone: +44 20 7403 6515

#492
Garfunkels Restaurants
Category: British, American
Average price: Inexpensive
Area: Westminster
Address: 2-3 Northumberland Avenue
London WC2N 5BY, UK
Phone: +44 20 7839 5148

#493
Barbican Pit Theatre
Category: Performing Arts
Area: Barbican
Address: Barbican Centre
London EC2Y 8DS, UK
Phone: +44 20 7638 4141

#494
Whitechapel Sports Centre
Category: Leisure Center
Area: Whitechapel
Address: 55 Durward Street
London E1 5BA, UK
Phone: +44 20 7247 7538

#495
St.George's Pool
Category: Swimming Pool
Address: 221 The Highway
London E1W 3BP, UK
Phone: +44 20 7709 9714

#496
Martens Airwair International
Category: Shoe Store
Average price: Expensive
Area: Covent Garden
Address: 17-19 Neal Street
London WC2H 9PU, UK
Phone: +44 20 7240 7555

#497
Brixton Recreation Centre
Category: Leisure Center, Gym
Area: Coldharbour Lane/ Herne Hill
Address: 27 Brixton Station Road
London SW9 8QQ, UK
Phone: +44 20 7926 9779

#498
Ferry Boat Inn
Category: Pub, Burgers
Area: Walthamstow, Tottenham
Address: Ferry Lane
London N17 9NG, UK
Phone: +44 20 8808 4980

#499
Little Heroes
Category: Toy Store
Average price: Expensive
Area: Fulham
Address: 638 Fulham Road
London SW6 5RT, UK
Phone: +44 20 7348 7907

#500
Giraffe
Category: Burgers
Average price: Modest
Area: Stratford, Olympic Village
Address: 304-305 The Loft
London E20 1ET, UK
Phone: +44 20 8536 0335

CPSIA information can be obtained
at www.ICGtesting.com
Printed in the USA
BVHW040228101218
535218BV00020B/705/P

9 781544 980164